Sweet Stripes for baby

Count to three when you choose the colors for these sweet baby wraps. Each features a different fun pattern stitch that lets you work with only one color at a time. But because the unused colors in each row are carried along the edge, there are no loose ends to hide later.

LEISURE ARTS, INC. • Maumelle, Arkansas

Playful Ripple

EASY +

Finished Size: 33½" x 43" (85 cm x 109 cm)

SHOPPING LIST

Yarn (Light Weight) LIGHT 3

[5 ounces, 362 yards

(140 grams, 331 meters) per skein**]**:

- ☐ White - 2 skeins
- ☐ Yellow - 2 skeins
- ☐ Green - 2 skeins

Crochet Hook

- ☐ Size H (5 mm)

  or size needed for gauge

GAUGE INFORMATION

In pattern, one repeat = 5½" (14 cm);

9 rows (Rows 7-15) = 4" (10 cm)

See Measuring Your Ripple Gauge & Ripple Afghan, page 29.

Gauge Swatch:

11"w x 4½"h (28 cm x 11.5 cm)

With White, ch 49.

Work same as Body Rows 1-9, pages 4 and 5: 32 dc and 16 ch-1 sps.

Finish off; cut White and Yellow.

STITCH GUIDE

DOUBLE CROCHET 2 TOGETHER

(abbreviated dc2tog) (uses next 2 ch-1 sps)

★ YO, insert hook in **next** ch-1 sp, YO and pull up a loop, YO and draw through 2 loops on hook; repeat from ★ once **more**, YO and draw through all 3 loops on hook **(counts as one dc)**.

INSTRUCTIONS

Body

With White, ch 149; place marker in second ch from hook for Edging placement.

Row 1: Hdc in second ch from hook and in next 10 chs, 3 hdc in next ch, hdc in next 11 chs, ★ skip next 2 chs, hdc in next 11 chs, 3 hdc in next ch, hdc in next 11 chs; repeat from ★ across changing to Yellow in last hdc ***(Fig. 1b, page 30)***, do **not** cut White: 150 hdc.

At the end of each row, do **not** cut previous color unless specified. Unused colors are carried loosely along the sides and are crocheted over when working the Edging.

Row 2 (Right side)**:** Ch 2, turn; skip first hdc, hdc in next 11 hdc, 3 hdc in next hdc, ★ hdc in next 11 hdc, skip next 2 hdc, hdc in next 11 hdc, 3 hdc in next hdc; repeat from ★ across to last 12 hdc, hdc in next 10 hdc, skip next hdc, hdc in last hdc changing to Green.

Note: Loop a short piece of yarn around any stitch to mark Row 2 as **right** side.

Row 3: Ch 2, turn; skip first hdc, hdc in next 11 hdc, 3 hdc in next hdc, ★ hdc in next 11 hdc, skip next 2 hdc, hdc in next 11 hdc, 3 hdc in next hdc; repeat from ★ across to last 12 hdc, hdc in next 10 hdc, skip next hdc, hdc in last hdc changing to White.

Continue working in the following stripe sequence: One row **each**, ★ White, Yellow, Green; repeat from ★ for sequence.

Rows 4-6: Ch 2, turn; skip first hdc, hdc in next 11 hdc, 3 hdc in next hdc, ★ hdc in next 11 hdc, skip next 2 hdc, hdc in next 11 hdc, 3 hdc in next hdc; repeat from ★ across to last 12 hdc, hdc in next 10 hdc, skip next hdc, hdc in last hdc changing to next color.

Row 7: Ch 2, turn; skip first 2 hdc, (dc, ch 1, dc) in next hdc, **[**skip next 2 hdc, (dc, ch 1, dc) in next hdc**]** twice, skip next hdc, (dc, ch 1, dc) in next hdc, skip next hdc, (dc, ch 2, dc) in next hdc, skip next hdc, (dc, ch 1, dc) in next hdc, ★ **[**skip next 2 hdc, (dc, ch 1, dc) in next hdc**]** 7 times, skip next hdc, (dc, ch 2, dc) in next hdc, skip next hdc, (dc, ch 1, dc) in next hdc; repeat from ★ across to last 10 hdc, skip next hdc, (dc, ch 1, dc) in next hdc, **[**skip next 2 hdc, (dc, ch 1, dc) in next hdc**]** twice, skip next hdc, dc in last hdc changing to next color ***(Fig. 1c, page 30)***: 109 dc and 54 sps.

Row 8: Ch 2, turn; skip first 2 dc, dc in next ch-1 sp, (dc, ch 1, dc) in each of next 3 ch-1 sps, (dc, ch 2, dc) in next ch-2 sp, (dc, ch 1, dc) in each of next 3 ch-1 sps, ★ dc2tog, (dc, ch 1, dc) in each of next 3 ch-1 sps, (dc, ch 2, dc) in next ch-2 sp, (dc, ch 1, dc) in each of next 3 ch-1 sps; repeat from ★ across to last ch-1 sp, YO, insert hook in last ch-1 sp, YO and pull up a loop, YO and draw through 2 loops on hook, YO, insert hook in top of turning ch, YO and pull up a loop, YO and draw through 2 loops on hook, YO and draw through all 3 loops on hook with next color **(counts as one dc)**: 91 dc and 42 sps.

Row 9: Ch 2, turn; (dc, ch 1, dc) in each of next 3 ch-1 sps, dc in next ch-2 sp, (ch 1, dc in same sp) twice, (dc, ch 1, dc) in each of next 3 ch-1 sps, ★ skip next dc, dc in next dc, (dc, ch 1, dc) in each of next 3 ch-1 sps, dc in next ch-2 sp, (ch 1, dc in same sp) twice, (dc, ch 1, dc) in each of next 3 ch-1 sps; repeat from ★ across to last 2 dc, skip last 2 dc, dc in top of turning ch changing to next color: 96 dc and 48 sps.

Row 10: Ch 2, turn; skip first dc, hdc in next dc and in next ch-1 sp, (hdc in next 2 dc and in next ch-1 sp) 3 times, 3 hdc in next dc, hdc in next ch-1 sp, (hdc in next 2 dc and in next ch-1 sp) 3 times, ★ hdc in next dc, skip next dc, hdc in next dc and in next ch-1 sp, (hdc in next 2 dc and in next ch-1 sp) 3 times, 3 hdc in next dc, hdc in next ch-1 sp, (hdc in next 2 dc and in next ch-1 sp) 3 times; repeat from ★ across to last dc, skip last dc, hdc in top of turning ch changing to next color: 150 hdc.

Rows 11-15: Ch 2, turn; skip first hdc, hdc in next 11 hdc, 3 hdc in next hdc, ★ hdc in next 11 hdc, skip next 2 hdc, hdc in next 11 hdc, 3 hdc in next hdc; repeat from ★ across to last 12 hdc, hdc in next 10 hdc, skip next hdc, hdc in last hdc changing to next color.

Repeat Rows 7-15 for pattern until piece measures approximately 42½" (108 cm), ending by working a Yellow hdc row as a **wrong** side row; cut Yellow and White ONLY.

Edging

With Green, ch 2, turn; skip first hdc, hdc in next 11 hdc, 3 hdc in next hdc, ★ hdc in next 11 hdc, skip next 2 hdc, hdc in next 11 hdc, 3 hdc in next hdc; repeat from ★ across to last 12 hdc, hdc in next 10 hdc, skip next hdc, 3 hdc in last hdc; working in end of rows, hdc evenly across; working in free loops of beginning ch *(Fig. 2, page 30)*, 3 hdc in marked ch, remove marker, hdc in next 10 chs, [skip next ch, hdc in next 11 chs, 3 hdc in next ch-2 sp, hdc in next 11 chs] across to last 12 chs, skip next ch, hdc in next 10 chs, 3 hdc in last ch; working in end of rows, hdc evenly across; 3 hdc in first hdc; join with slip st to first hdc, finish off.

Berry Patch

EASY +

Finished Size: 31" x 41" (78.5 cm x 104 cm)

SHOPPING LIST

Yarn (Light Weight) 3

[5 ounces, 362 yards
(140 grams, 331 meters) per skein]:

- ☐ Pink - 2 skeins
- ☐ White - 2 skeins
- ☐ Lavender - 2 skeins

Crochet Hook

- ☐ Size G (4 mm)
  or size needed for gauge

GAUGE INFORMATION

In pattern, 16 sts = 4" (10 cm); 18 rows (Rows 2-19) = 3¾" (9.5 cm)

Gauge Swatch:
4¼"w x 4"h (10.75 cm x 10 cm)

With White, ch 18.

Work same as Body Rows 1-19, page 8: 17 sc.

Finish off; cut Pink and Lavender.

STITCH GUIDE

BLACKBERRY STITCH

(abbreviated Blackberry St) (uses one sc)

Insert hook in sc indicated, YO and pull up a loop (2 loops on hook), (YO and draw through one loop on hook) 3 times, keeping ch toward you, YO and draw through both loops on hook.

INSTRUCTIONS

Body

With White, ch 120; place marker in second ch from hook for Edging placement.

Row 1: Sc in second ch from hook and in each ch across changing to Lavender in last sc ***(Fig. 1a, page 30)***; do **not** cut White: 119 sc.

At the end of each row, do **not** cut previous color unless specified. Unused colors are carried loosely along the sides and are crocheted over when working the Edging.

Row 2 (Right side)**:** Ch 1, turn; sc in first sc, (work Blackberry St in next sc, sc in next sc) across changing to Pink in last sc: 60 sc and 59 Blackberry Sts.

Continue working in the following stripe sequence: One row **each**, ★ Pink, White, Lavender; repeat from ★ for sequence.

Rows 3-5: Ch 1, turn; sc in each st across changing to next color in last sc: 119 sc.

Row 6: Ch 1, turn; sc in first sc, (work Blackberry St in next sc, sc in next sc) across changing to next color in last sc: 60 sc and 59 Blackberry Sts.

Rows 7-10: Repeat Rows 3-6: 60 sc and 59 Blackberry Sts.

Rows 11-19: Ch 1, turn; sc in each st across changing to next color in last sc: 119 sc.

Row 20: Ch 1, turn; sc in first sc, (work Blackberry St in next sc, sc in next sc) across changing to next color in last sc: 60 sc and 59 Blackberry Sts.

Rows 21-191: Repeat Rows 3-20, 9 times; then repeat Rows 3-11 once **more**; cut White and Lavender ONLY: 119 sc.

Edging

Rnd 1 (Right side)**:** With Pink, ch 1, turn; 2 sc in first sc, sc in each sc across to last sc, 3 sc in last sc; work 157 sc evenly spaced across end of rows; working in free loops of beginning ch ***(Fig. 2, page 30)***, 3 sc in marked ch, remove marker, sc in each ch across to last ch, 3 sc in last ch; work 157 sc evenly spaced across end of rows; sc in same st as first sc; join with slip st to first sc: 560 sc.

Rnd 2: Ch 1, do **not** turn; sc in same st as joining, 3 dc in next sc, sc in next sc, ★ (skip next sc, 3 dc in next sc, skip next sc, sc in next sc) across to next corner 3-sc group, (3 dc in next sc, sc in next sc) twice; repeat from ★ 2 times **more**, (skip next sc, 3 dc in next sc, skip next sc, sc in next sc) across to last sc, 3 dc in last sc; join with slip st to first sc, finish off.

Bouncing Baby

EASY +

Finished Size: 32" x 42½" (81.5 cm x 108 cm)

SHOPPING LIST

Yarn (Medium Weight) MEDIUM 4

[6 ounces, 315 yards (170.1 grams, 288 meters) per skein**]**:

- ☐ Off White - 2 skeins
- ☐ Lavender - 2 skeins
- ☐ Purple - 2 skeins

Crochet Hook

- ☐ Size H (5 mm)
  or size needed for gauge

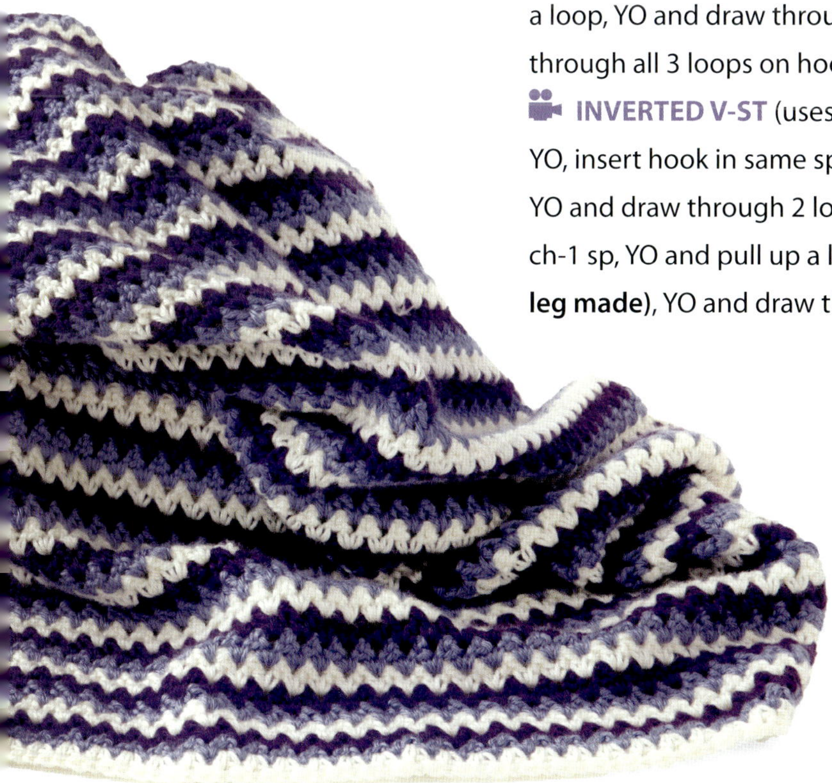

GAUGE INFORMATION

In pattern, nine repeats (18 sts) = 5" (12.75 cm); 9 rows = 4½" (11.5 cm)

Gauge Swatch:

5½"w x 4½"h (14 cm x 11.5 cm)

With Lavender, ch 21.

Work same as Body, page 10, for 9 rows: 20 sts.

Finish off; cut Lavender and Purple.

STITCH GUIDE

BEGINNING INVERTED V-ST (uses first 2 ch-1 sps)

YO, insert hook in first ch-1 sp, YO and pull up a loop, YO and draw through 2 loops on hook **(first leg made)**, YO, insert hook in next ch-1 sp, YO and pull up a loop, YO and draw through 2 loops on hook **(second leg made)**, YO and draw through all 3 loops on hook.

INVERTED V-ST (uses 2 ch-1 sps)

YO, insert hook in same sp as second leg of previous st, YO and pull up a loop, YO and draw through 2 loops on hook **(first leg made)**, YO, insert hook in next ch-1 sp, YO and pull up a loop, YO and draw through 2 loops on hook **(second leg made)**, YO and draw through all 3 loops on hook.

INSTRUCTIONS

Body

With Lavender, ch 113.

Row 1: YO, insert hook in third ch from hook **(2 skipped chs count as first sp)**, YO and pull up a loop, YO and draw through 2 loops on hook **(first leg made)**, YO, skip next ch, insert hook in next ch, YO and pull up a loop, YO and draw through 2 loops on hook **(second leg made)**, YO and draw through all 3 loops on hook, ch 1, ★ YO, insert hook in same ch as second leg of previous st, YO and pull up a loop, YO and draw through 2 loops on hook **(first leg made)**, YO, skip next ch, insert hook in next ch, YO and pull up a loop, YO and draw through 2 loops on hook **(second leg made)**, YO and draw through all 3 loops on hook, ch 1; repeat from ★ across, dc in same ch as second leg of previous st changing to Purple ***(Fig. 1c, page 30)***; do **not** cut Lavender: 56 sts and 56 sps.

At the end of each row, do **not** cut previous color unless specified. Unused colors are carried loosely along the sides and are crocheted over when working the Edging.

Row 2 (Right side)**:** Ch 2 **(counts as first sp, now and throughout)**, turn; work beginning Inverted V-St, ch 1, (work Inverted V-St, ch 1) across, dc in same sp as second leg of last Inverted V-St changing to Off White.

Note: Loop a short piece of yarn around any stitch to mark Row 2 as **right** side.

Row 3: Ch 2, turn; work beginning Inverted V-St, ch 1, (work Inverted V-St, ch 1) across, dc in same sp as second leg of last Inverted V-St changing to Lavender.

Row 4: Ch 2, turn; work beginning Inverted V-St, ch 1, (work Inverted V-St, ch 1) across, dc in same sp as second leg of last Inverted V-St changing to Purple.

Row 5: Ch 2, turn; work beginning Inverted V-St, ch 1, (work Inverted V-St, ch 1) across, dc in same sp as second leg of last Inverted V-St changing to Off White.

Repeat Rows 3-5 for pattern until piece measures approximately 41½" (105.5 cm) from beginning ch, ending by working Row 5 as a **wrong** side row; cut Lavender and Purple ONLY.

Edging

With Off White, ch 2, turn; work beginning Inverted V-St, ch 1, (work Inverted V-St, ch 1) across, 3 dc in same sp as second leg of last Inverted V-St, ch 1; † working in sp at end of each row, work (Inverted V-St, ch 1) across, 3 dc in same sp as second leg of last Inverted V-St, ch 1 †; working in sps across beginning ch, (work Inverted V-St, ch 1) across ending with second leg of last Inverted V-St in sp **before** last dc, ch 1, 3 dc in same sp as second leg of last Inverted V-St, ch 1; repeat from † to † once; join with slip st to top of beginning ch-2, finish off.

Waffled Warmth

EASY +

Finished Size: 33" x 42½" (84 cm x 108 cm)

SHOPPING LIST

Yarn (Medium Weight)

MEDIUM 4

[16 ounces, 1,020 yards
(454 grams, 932 meters) per skein**]**:

- ☐ White - 2/3 skein
- ☐ Lavender - 2/3 skein
- ☐ Peach - 2/3 skein

Crochet Hook

- ☐ Size I (5.5 mm)
  or size needed for gauge

GAUGE INFORMATION

In pattern, 15 sts = 4" (10 cm);
12 rows = 4½" (11.5 cm)

Gauge Swatch:
4¼"w 4½"h (10.75 cm x 11.5 cm)

With White, ch 18.

Work same as Body, page 14, for 12 rows: 16 sts.

Finish off; cut White and Lavender.

STITCH GUIDE

FRONT POST DOUBLE CROCHET ***(abbreviated FPdc)***

YO, insert hook from **front** to **back** around post of st indicated, YO and pull up a loop (3 loops on hook) ***(Fig. A)***, (YO and draw through 2 loops on hook) twice.

Fig. A

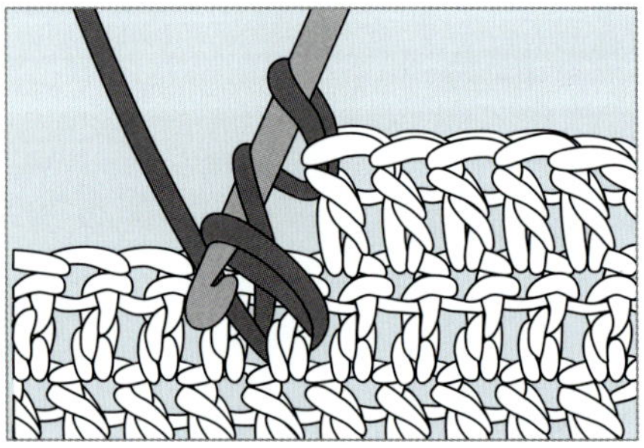

INSTRUCTIONS

Body

With White, ch 122; place marker in third ch from hook for Edging placement.

Row 1 (Right side)**:** Dc in fourth ch from hook **(3 skipped chs count as first dc)** and in each ch across changing to Lavender in last dc *(Fig. 1c, page 30)*; do **not** cut White: 120 dc.

At the end of each row, do **not** cut previous color unless specified. Unused colors are carried loosely along the sides and are crocheted over when working the Edging.

Note: Loop a short piece of yarn around any stitch to mark Row 1 as **right** side.

Row 2: Ch 3 **(counts as first dc, now and throughout)**, turn; work FPdc around next dc, (dc in next dc, work FPdc around next dc) across to last 2 dc, dc in last 2 dc changing to Peach in last dc.

Row 3: Ch 3, turn; work FPdc around next dc, (dc in next st, work FPdc around next dc) across to last 2 sts, dc in last sts changing to White in last dc.

Row 4: Ch 3, turn; work FPdc around next dc, (dc in next st, work FPdc around next dc) across to last 2 sts, dc in last 2 sts changing to Lavender in last dc.

Row 5: Ch 3, turn; work FPdc around next dc, (dc in next st, work FPdc around next dc) across to last 2 sts, dc in last 2 sts changing to Peach in last dc.

Repeat Rows 3-5 for pattern until piece measures approximately 41½" (105.5 cm) from beginning ch, ending by working Row 3 as a **right** side row; cut Lavender and Peach ONLY.

Edging

Rnd 1: With **right** side facing and White, ch 1, 2 sc in last sc made; sc evenly across end of rows; working in free loops of beginning ch *(Fig. 2, page 30)*, 3 sc in first ch, sc in each ch across to marked ch, 3 sc in marked ch, remove marker; sc evenly across end of rows; working in sts across last row, 3 sc in first dc, sc in each st across and in same st as first sc; join with slip st to first sc.

Rnd 2: Ch 2, 2 hdc in same st as joining, hdc in next sc and in each sc around working 3 hdc in center sc of each corner 3-sc group; join with slip st to top of beginning ch-2, finish off.

Baby Shells

EASY +

Finished Size: 31" x 43" (78.5 cm x 109 cm)

SHOPPING LIST

Yarn (Medium Weight) MEDIUM 4

[6 ounces, 315 yards

(170.1 grams, 288 meters) per skein]:

- ☐ Gold - 2 skeins
- ☐ Lt Blue - 2 skeins
- ☐ Blue - 2 skeins

Crochet Hook

- ☐ Size H (5 mm)

  or size needed for gauge

GAUGE INFORMATION

In pattern, (sc, ch 1, dc) 6 times = 4" (10 cm); 15 rows = 4½" (11.5 cm)

Gauge Swatch:

4¾"w x 5½"h (12 cm x 14 cm)

With Lt Blue, ch 15.

Work same as Body, page 16, for 18 rows: 14 sts and 7 chs.

Finish off; cut Lt Blue and Blue.

INSTRUCTIONS

Body

With Lt Blue, ch 91.

Row 1 (Right side)**:** Sc in second ch from hook and in each ch across changing to Blue in last sc ***(Fig. 1a, page 30)***; do **not** cut Lt Blue: 90 sc.

At the end of each row, do **not** cut previous color unless specified. Unused colors are carried loosely along the sides and are crocheted over when working the Edging.

Note: Loop a short piece of yarn around any stitch to mark Row 1 as **right** side.

Row 2: Ch 1, turn; skip first sc, (sc, ch 1, dc) in next sc, ★ skip next sc, (sc, ch 1, dc) in next sc; repeat from ★ across changing to Gold in last dc ***(Fig. 1c, page 30)***: 90 sts and 45 chs.

Row 3: Ch 1, turn; skip first dc and next ch, (sc, ch 1, dc) in next sc, ★ skip next dc and next ch, (sc, ch 1, dc) in next sc; repeat from ★ across changing to Lt Blue in last dc.

Row 4: Ch 1, turn; skip first dc and next ch, (sc, ch 1, dc) in next sc, ★ skip next dc and next ch, (sc, ch 1, dc) in next sc; repeat from ★ across changing to Blue in last dc.

Row 5: Ch 1, turn; skip first dc and next ch, (sc, ch 1, dc) in next sc, ★ skip next dc and next ch, (sc, ch 1, dc) in next sc; repeat from ★ across changing to Gold in last dc.

Repeat Rows 3-5 for pattern until piece measures approximately 42" (106.5 cm) from beginning ch, ending by working Row 5 as a **wrong** side row; cut Lt Blue and Blue ONLY.

Edging

Rnd 1: With Gold, ch 1, turn; skip first dc and next ch, (sc, ch 1, dc) in next sc, ★ skip next dc and next ch, (sc, ch 1, dc) in next sc; repeat from ★ across; working in end of rows, skip first row, (sc, ch 1, dc) in next row, **[**skip next row, (sc, ch 1, dc) in next row**]** across; working around beginning ch, (sc, ch 1, dc) in top of each sc worked into on Row 1; working in end of rows, skip first row, (sc, ch 1, dc) in next row, **[**skip next row, (sc, ch 1, dc) in next row**]** across; join with slip st to first sc.

Rnd 2: Ch 1, do **not** turn; (sc, ch 1, dc) in same st as joining, skip next ch and next dc, ★ (sc, ch 1, dc) in next sc, skip next ch and next dc; repeat from ★ around; join with slip st to first sc, finish off.

Bobbling Along

EASY +

Finished Size: 33" x 47¾" (84 cm x 121.5 cm)

SHOPPING LIST

Yarn (Light Weight) LIGHT 3

[12.3 ounces, 1,256 yards

(350 grams, 1,148 meters) per skein**]**:

- ☐ White - 2/3 skein
- ☐ Lt Blue - 2/3 skein
- ☐ Peach - 2/3 skein

Crochet Hook

- ☐ Size H (5 mm)

  or size needed for gauge

GAUGE INFORMATION

In pattern, one repeat (25 sts from point-to-point) = 4⅛" (10.5 cm);

16 rows = 4¾" (12 cm)

See Measuring Your Ripple Gauge & Ripple Afghan, page 29.

Gauge Swatch:

8¼"w x 3"h (21 cm x 7.5 cm)

With White, ch 48.

Work same as Body Rows 1-10, page 20: 50 sc.

Finish off; cut Lt Blue and Peach.

STITCH GUIDE

BOBBLE (uses one st or sp)

★ YO, insert hook in st or sp indicated, YO and pull up a loop, YO and draw through 2 loops on hook; repeat from ★ 4 times **more**, YO and draw through all 6 loops on hook.

INSTRUCTIONS

Body

With White, ch 192.

Row 1 (Right side)**:** Sc in second ch from hook and in next 10 chs, 3 sc in next ch, sc in next 11 chs, ★ skip next ch, sc in next 11 chs, 3 sc in next ch, sc in next 11 chs; repeat from ★ across changing to Lt Blue in last sc ***(Fig. 1a, page 30)***; do **not** cut White: 200 sc.

At the end of each row, do **not** cut previous color unless specified. Unused colors are carried loosely along the sides and are crocheted over when working the Edging.

Row 2: Ch 1, turn; skip first sc, sc in next sc, (ch 1, skip next sc, sc in next sc) 5 times, 3 sc in next sc, sc in next sc, ★ (ch 1, skip next sc, sc in next sc) 5 times, skip next 2 sc, sc in next sc, (ch 1, skip next sc, sc in next sc) 5 times, 3 sc in next sc, sc in next sc; repeat from ★ across to last 11 sc, (ch 1, skip next sc, sc in next sc) 4 times, ch 1, skip next 2 sc, sc in last sc changing to Peach: 120 sc and 80 ch-1 sps.

Row 3: Ch 1, turn; skip first sc, (sc in next ch-1 sp, ch 1) 5 times, skip next sc, sc in next sc, 3 sc in next sc, sc in next sc, ★ (ch 1, sc in next ch-1 sp) 5 times, skip next 2 sc, (sc in next ch-1 sp, ch 1) 5 times, skip next sc, sc in next sc, 3 sc in next sc, sc in next sc; repeat from ★ across to last 5 ch-1 sps, (ch 1, sc in next ch-1 sp) 4 times, ch 1, skip next ch-1 sp, sc in last sc changing to White.

Continue working in the following stripe sequence: One row **each**, ★ White, Lt Blue, Peach; repeat from ★ for sequence.

Rows 4-8: Ch 1, turn; skip first sc, (sc in next ch-1 sp, ch 1) 5 times, skip next sc, sc in next sc, 3 sc in next sc, sc in next sc, ★ (ch 1, sc in next ch-1 sp) 5 times, skip next 2 sc, (sc in next ch-1 sp, ch 1) 5 times, skip next sc, sc in next sc, 3 sc in next sc, sc in next sc; repeat from ★ across to last 5 ch-1 sps, (ch 1, sc in next ch-1 sp) 4 times, ch 1, skip next ch-1 sp, sc in last sc changing to next color.

Row 9: Ch 1, turn; skip first sc, ★ † sc in next ch-1 sp and in next sc, work Bobble in next ch-1 sp, sc in next sc and in next ch-1 sp, work Bobble in next sc, sc in next ch-1 sp and in next sc, work Bobble in next ch-1 sp, sc in next 2 sc, (sc, work Bobble, sc) in next sc, sc in next 2 sc, work Bobble in next ch-1 sp, sc in next sc and in next ch-1 sp, work Bobble in next sc, sc in next ch-1 sp and in next sc, work Bobble in next ch-1 sp †, sc in next sc and in next ch-1 sp, skip next 2 sc; repeat from ★ 6 times **more**, then repeat from † to † once, sc in next sc, skip next ch-1 sp, sc in last sc changing to next color: 200 sts (144 sc and 56 Bobbles).

Row 10: Ch 1, turn; skip first sc, sc in next 11 sts, 3 sc in next Bobble, ★ sc in next 11 sts, skip next 2 sc, sc in next 11 sts, 3 sc in next Bobble; repeat from ★ across to last 12 sts, sc in next 10 sts, skip next sc, sc in last sc changing to next color.

Row 11: Ch 1, turn; skip first sc, sc in next sc, (ch 1, skip next sc, sc in next sc) 5 times, 3 sc in next sc, sc in next sc, ★ (ch 1, skip next sc, sc in next sc) 5 times, skip next 2 sc, sc in next sc, (ch 1, skip next sc, sc in next sc) 5 times, 3 sc in next sc, sc in next sc; repeat from ★ across to last 11 sc, (ch 1, skip next sc, sc in next sc) 4 times, ch 1, skip next 2 sc, sc in last sc changing to next color: 120 sc and 80 ch-1 sps.

Rows 12-147: Repeat Rows 4-11, 17 times: 120 sc and 80 ch-1 sps.

Rows 148-154: Ch 1, turn; skip first sc, (sc in next ch-1 sp, ch 1) 5 times, skip next sc, sc in next sc, 3 sc in next sc, sc in next sc, ★ (ch 1, sc in next ch-1 sp) 5 times, skip next 2 sc, (sc in next ch-1 sp, ch 1) 5 times, skip next sc, sc in next sc, 3 sc in next sc, sc in next sc; repeat from ★ across to last 5 ch-1 sps, (ch 1, sc in next ch-1 sp) 4 times, ch 1, skip next ch-1 sp, sc in last sc changing to next color: 200 sts (120 sc and 80 ch-1 sps).

Cut White and Peach ONLY.

Edging

With Lt Blue, ch 1, turn; skip first sc, ★ † sc in next ch-1 sp, (sc in next sc and in next ch-1 sp) 4 times, sc in next 2 sc, 3 sc in next sc, sc in next 2 sc and in next ch-1 sp, (sc in next sc and in next ch-1 sp) 4 times †, skip next 2 sc; repeat from ★ 6 times **more**, then repeat from † to † once, 3 sc in last sc; sc in end of each row across; working in free loops of beginning ch *(Fig. 2, page 30)*, 3 sc in first ch, sc in next 10 chs, [skip next ch, sc in next 11 chs, 3 sc in next ch, sc in next 11 chs] 7 times, skip next ch, sc in next 10 chs, 3 sc in next ch; sc in end of each row across; 3 sc in first sc on Row 154; join with slip st to first sc, finish off.

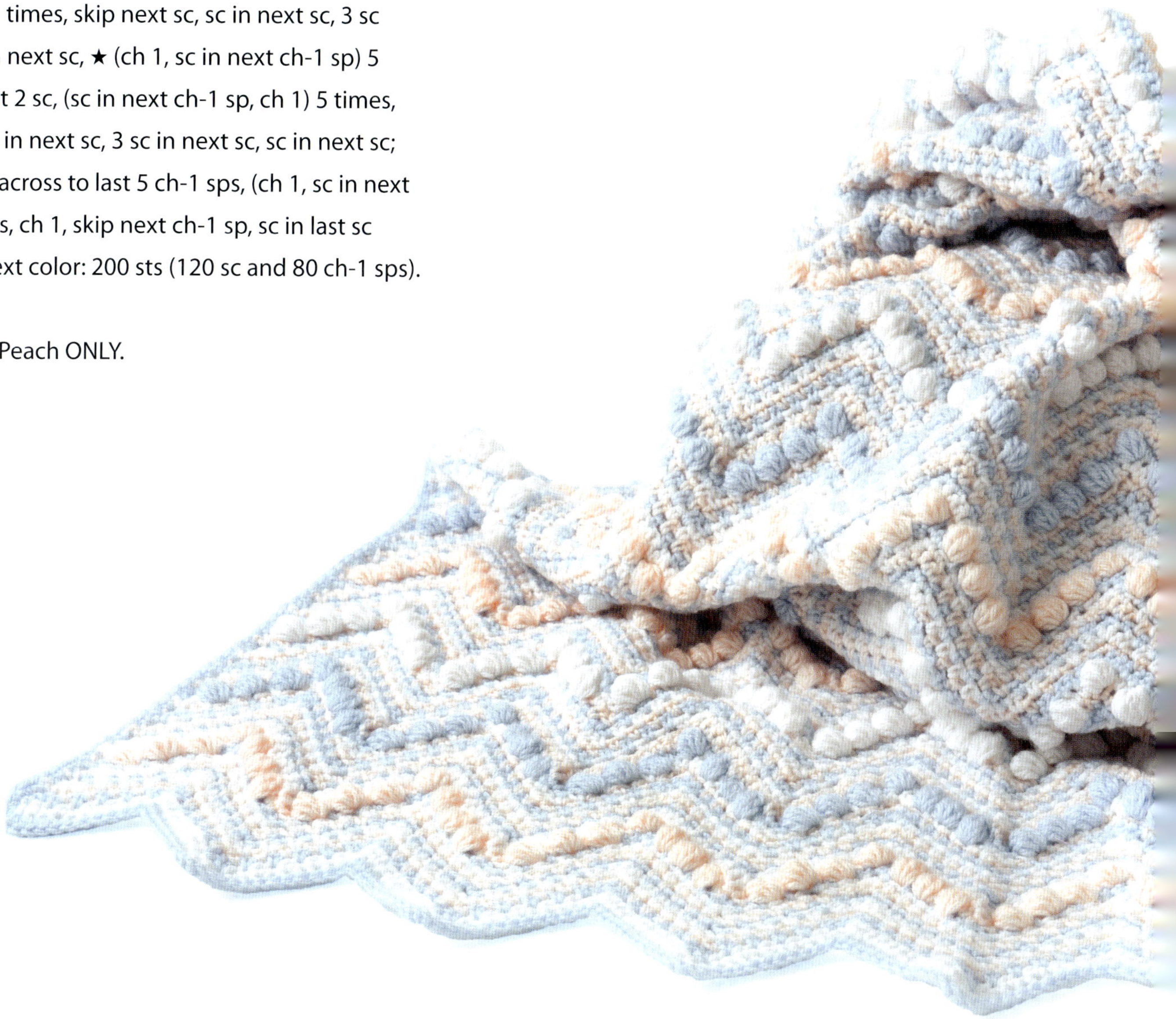

Gentle Waves

EASY +

Finished Size: 34½" x 44½" (87.5 cm x 113 cm)

SHOPPING LIST

Yarn (Medium Weight) 4

[6 ounces, 315 yards
(170.1 grams, 288 meters) per skein]:

- ☐ Teal - 2 skeins
- ☐ White - 2 skeins
- ☐ Aqua - 2 skeins

Crochet Hook

- ☐ Size H (5 mm)
  or size needed for gauge

GAUGE INFORMATION

In pattern, two repeats (20 sts) = 6" (15.25 cm); 9 rows = 4¾" (12 cm)

See Measuring Your Ripple Gauge & Ripple Afghan, page 29.

Gauge Swatch:

6¼"w x 4¾"h (16 cm x 12 cm)

With White, ch 22.

Work same as Body, page 24, for 9 rows: 21 sts.

Finish off; cut White and Aqua.

STITCH GUIDE

DOUBLE CROCHET 2 TOGETHER

(abbreviated dc2tog) (uses next 2 sts)

★ YO, insert hook in **next** st, YO and pull up a loop, YO and draw through 2 loops on hook; repeat from ★ once **more**, YO and draw through all 3 loops on hook **(counts as one dc)**.

INSTRUCTIONS

Body

With White, ch 112; place marker in second ch from hook for Edging placement.

Row 1 (Right side)**:** Dc2tog beginning in third ch from hook **(2 skipped chs count as first st)**, dc in next ch, (2 dc in next ch, dc in next ch) twice, ★ (dc2tog, dc in next ch) twice, (2 dc in next ch, dc in next ch) twice; repeat from ★ across to last 3 chs, dc2tog, dc in last ch changing to Aqua *(Fig. 1c, page 30)*; do **not** cut White: 111 sts.

At the end of each row, do **not** cut previous color unless specified. Unused colors are carried loosely along the sides and are crocheted over when working the Edging.

Note: Loop a short piece of yarn around any stitch to mark Row 1 as **right** side.

Row 2: Ch 2 **(counts as first st, now and throughout)**, turn; dc2tog, dc in next dc, (2 dc in next dc, dc in next dc) twice, ★ (dc2tog, dc in next dc) twice, (2 dc in next dc, dc in next dc) twice; repeat from ★ across to last 3 sts, dc2tog, dc in last st changing to Teal.

Row 3: Ch 2, turn; dc2tog, dc in next dc, (2 dc in next dc, dc in next dc) twice, ★ (dc2tog, dc in next dc) twice, (2 dc in next dc, dc in next dc) twice; repeat from ★ across to last 3 sts, dc2tog, dc in last st changing to White.

Row 4: Ch 2, turn; dc2tog, dc in next dc, (2 dc in next dc, dc in next dc) twice, ★ (dc2tog, dc in next dc) twice, (2 dc in next dc, dc in next dc) twice; repeat from ★ across to last 3 sts, dc2tog, dc in last st changing to Aqua.

Row 5: Ch 2, turn; dc2tog, dc in next dc, (2 dc in next dc, dc in next dc) twice, ★ (dc2tog, dc in next dc) twice, (2 dc in next dc, dc in next dc) twice; repeat from ★ across to last 3 sts, dc2tog, dc in last st changing to Teal.

Repeat Rows 3-5 for pattern until piece measures approximately 43½" (110.5 cm) from beginning ch, ending by working Row 5 as a **wrong** side row; cut White and Aqua ONLY.

Edging

With Teal, ch 2, turn; dc2tog, dc in next dc, (2 dc in next dc, dc in next dc) twice, ★ (dc2tog, dc in next dc) twice, (2 dc in next dc, dc in next dc) twice; repeat from ★ across to last 3 sts, dc2tog, leave last st unworked; working in end of rows, work 3 dc in first row, dc evenly across to last row, work 3 dc in last row; working in free loops of beginning ch *(Fig. 2, page 30)*, skip first ch, dc in each ch across to marked ch, remove marker; working in end of rows, work 3 dc in first row, dc evenly across to last row, work 3 dc in last row; join with slip st to first dc, finish off.

Sweet Memories

EASY

Finished Size: 31" x 41½" (78.5 cm x 105.5 cm)

SHOPPING LIST

Yarn (Medium Weight) MEDIUM 4

[7 ounces, 426 yards

(197 grams, 389 meters) per skein]:

- ☐ Pink - 1 skein
- ☐ White - 1 skein
- ☐ Aqua - 1 skein

Crochet Hook

- ☐ Size I (5.5 mm)

  or size needed for gauge

GAUGE INFORMATION

In pattern, (2 dc, ch 2, sc) 4 times = 3¾" (9.5 cm); 9 rows = 4½" (11.5 cm)

Gauge Swatch:

5"w x 3"h (12.75 cm x 7.5 cm)

With White, ch 19.

Work same as Body, page 26, for 6 rows: 17 sts and 5 ch-2 sps.

Finish off; cut White and Aqua.

INSTRUCTIONS

Body

With White, ch 97; place marker in second ch from hook for Edging placement.

Row 1: (2 Dc, ch 2, sc) in fourth ch from hook **(3 skipped chs count as first st)**, ★ skip next 2 chs, (2 dc, ch 2, sc) in next ch; repeat from ★ across to last 3 chs, skip next 2 chs, sc in last ch changing to Aqua ***(Fig. 1a, page 30)***; do **not** cut White: 95 sts and 31 ch-2 sps.

At the end of each row, do **not** cut previous color unless specified. Unused colors are carried loosely along the sides and are crocheted over when working the Edging.

Row 2 (Right side)**:** Ch 2 **(counts as first st)**, turn; (2 dc, ch 2, sc) in each ch-2 sp across to last 3 sts, skip next 2 dc, sc in last st changing to Pink.

Note: Loop a short piece of yarn around any stitch to mark Row 2 as **right** side.

Row 3: Ch 2, turn; (2 dc, ch 2, sc) in each ch-2 sp across to last 3 sts, skip next 2 dc, sc in last st changing to White.

Row 4: Ch 2, turn; (2 dc, ch 2, sc) in each ch-2 sp across to last 3 sts, skip next 2 dc, sc in last st changing to Aqua.

Row 5: Ch 2, turn; (2 dc, ch 2, sc) in each ch-2 sp across to last 3 sts, skip next 2 dc, sc in last st changing to Pink.

Repeat Rows 3-5 for pattern until piece measures approximately 40" (101.5 cm) from beginning ch, ending by working Row 5 as a **right** side row; cut Aqua and White ONLY.

Edging

Rnd 1: With **right** side facing and Pink, ch 1, sc in last sc made; work 104 sc evenly spaced across end of rows to marked ch, 3 sc in marked ch, remove marker; working in skipped chs and in free loops of beginning ch ***(Fig. 2, page 30)***, sc in each ch across to last 2 chs, 2 sc in next ch, 3 sc in last ch; work 104 sc evenly spaced across end of rows; working in sts across last row, 3 sc in first st, (sc in next 2 dc and in next ch-2 sp) across, 2 sc in next sc and in same st as first sc; join with slip st to first sc: 410 sc.

Rnd 2: Ch 1, sc in same st as joining, [skip next 2 sc, (2 dc, ch 2, sc) in next sc] across to center sc of next corner 3-sc group, skip center sc, ★ (2 dc, ch 2, sc) in next sc, [skip next 2 sc, (2 dc, ch 2, sc) in next sc] across to center sc of next corner 3-sc group, skip center sc; repeat from ★ 2 times **more**, 2 dc in same st as first sc, ch 2; join with slip st to first sc, finish off.

General Instructions

ABBREVIATIONS

ch(s)	chain(s)
cm	centimeters
dc	double crochet(s)
dc2tog	double crochet 2 together
FPdc	Front Post double crochet(s)
hdc	half double crochet(s)
mm	millimeters
Rnd(s)	Round(s)
sc	single crochet(s)
sp(s)	space(s)
st(s)	stitch(es)
YO	yarn over

SYMBOLS & TERMS

★ — work instructions following ★ as many **more** times as indicated in addition to the first time.

† to † — work all instructions from first † to second † **as many** times as specified.

( ) or **[ ]** — work enclosed instructions **as many** times as specified by the number immediately following **or** work all enclosed instructions in the stitch or space indicated **or** contains explanatory remarks.

colon (:) — the number(s) given after a colon at the end of a row or round denote(s) the number of stitches or spaces you should have on that row or round.

GAUGE

Exact gauge is **essential** for proper size. Before beginning your Baby Afghan, make the sample swatch given in the individual instructions in the yarn and hook specified. After completing the swatch, measure it, counting your stitches and rows carefully. If your swatch is larger or smaller than specified, **make another, changing hook size to get the correct gauge.** Keep trying until you find the size hook that will give you the specified gauge.

CROCHET TERMINOLOGY		
UNITED STATES		INTERNATIONAL
slip stitch (slip st)	=	single crochet (sc)
single crochet (sc)	=	double crochet (dc)
half double crochet (hdc)	=	half treble crochet (htr)
double crochet (dc)	=	treble crochet (tr)
treble crochet (tr)	=	double treble crochet (dtr)
double treble crochet (dtr)	=	triple treble crochet (ttr)
triple treble crochet (tr tr)	=	quadruple treble crochet (qtr)
skip	=	miss

CROCHET HOOKS																	
U.S.	B-1	C-2	D-3	E-4	F-5	G-6	7	H-8	I-9	J-10	K-10½	L-11	M/N-13	N/P-15	P/Q	Q	S
Metric - mm	2.25	2.75	3.25	3.5	3.75	4	4.5	5	5.5	6	6.5	8	9	10	15	16	19

BEGINNER	Projects for first-time crocheters using basic stitches. Minimal shaping.
EASY	Projects using yarn with basic stitches, repetitive stitch patterns, simple color changes, and simple shaping and finishing.
INTERMEDIATE	Projects using a variety of techniques, such as basic lace patterns or color patterns, mid-level shaping and finishing.
EXPERIENCED	Projects with intricate stitch patterns, techniques and dimension, such as non-repeating patterns, multi-color techniques, fine threads, small hooks, detailed shaping and refined finishing.

MEASURING YOUR RIPPLE GAUGE & RIPPLE AFGHAN

Lay your piece on a flat, hard surface. Measure one point-to-point repeat by placing the ruler from the center of one "peak" increase to the center of the next "peak" increase.

Measure the height of your gauge swatch by placing the ruler from the bottom of the center stitch of a "peak" increase to the highest point of the swatch.

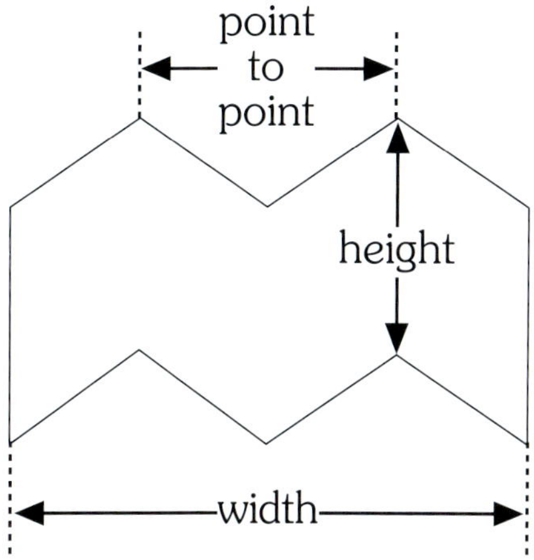

Measure the width of your gauge swatch or afghan from straight edge to straight edge. The length of the afghan is measured from the bottom of the lowest "valley" to the top of the highest "peak."

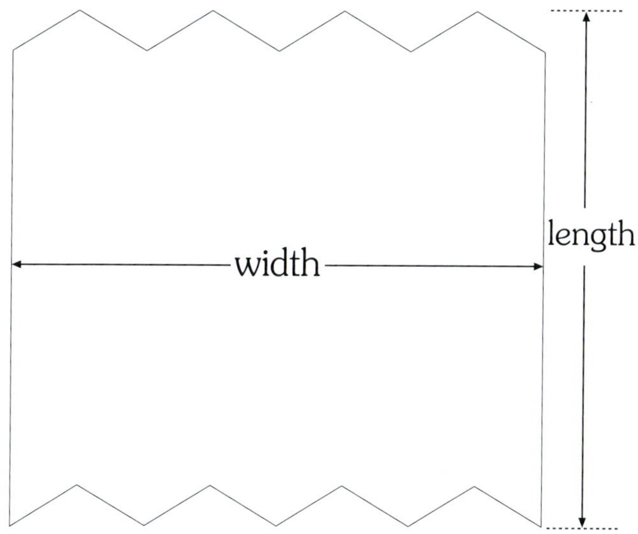

Yarn Weight Symbol & Names	LACE 0	SUPER FINE 1	FINE 2	LIGHT 3	MEDIUM 4	BULKY 5	SUPER BULKY 6	JUMBO 7
Type of Yarns in Category	Fingering, size 10 crochet thread	Sock, Fingering, Baby	Sport, Baby	DK, Light Worsted	Worsted, Afghan, Aran	Chunky, Craft, Rug	Super Bulky, Roving	Jumbo, Roving
Crochet Gauge* Ranges in Single Crochet to 4" (10 cm)	32-42 sts**	21-32 sts	16-20 sts	12-17 sts	11-14 sts	8-11 sts	6-9 sts	5 sts and fewer
Advised Hook Size Range	Steel*** 6 to 8, Regular hook B-1	B-1 to E-4	E-4 to 7	7 to I-9	I-9 to K-10½	K-10½ to M/N-13	M/N-13 to Q	Q and larger

*GUIDELINES ONLY: The chart above reflects the most commonly used gauges and hook sizes for specific yarn categories.

** Lace weight yarns are usually crocheted with larger hooks to create lacy openwork patterns. Accordingly, a gauge range is difficult to determine. Always follow the gauge stated in your pattern.

*** Steel crochet hooks are sized differently from regular hooks–the higher the number, the smaller the hook, which is the reverse of regular hook sizing.

CHANGING COLORS

Work the last stitch to within one step of completion, hook new yarn ***(Fig. 1a, b, or c)*** and draw through all loops on hook.

Fig. 1a

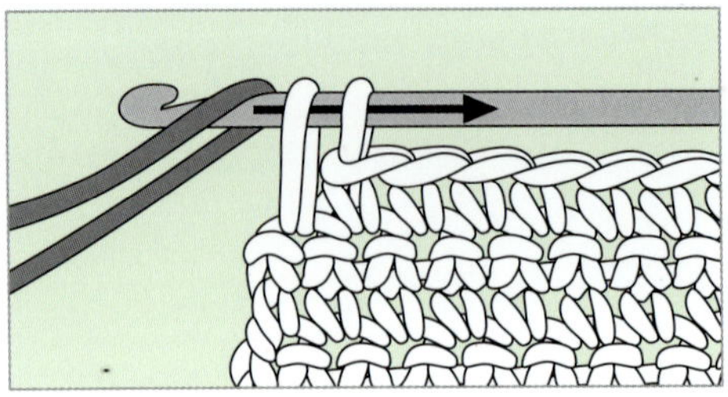

Fig. 1b

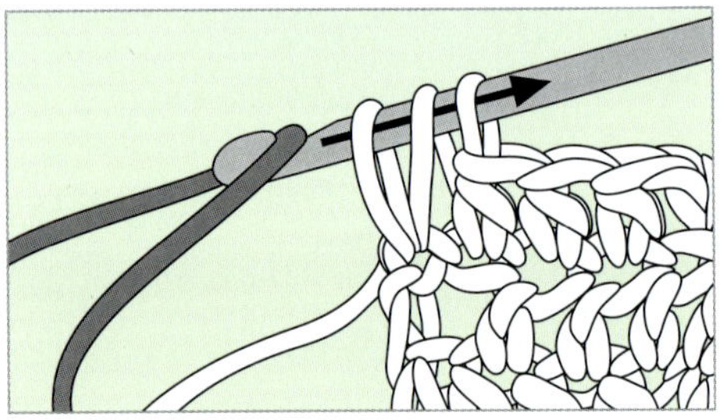

Fig. 1c

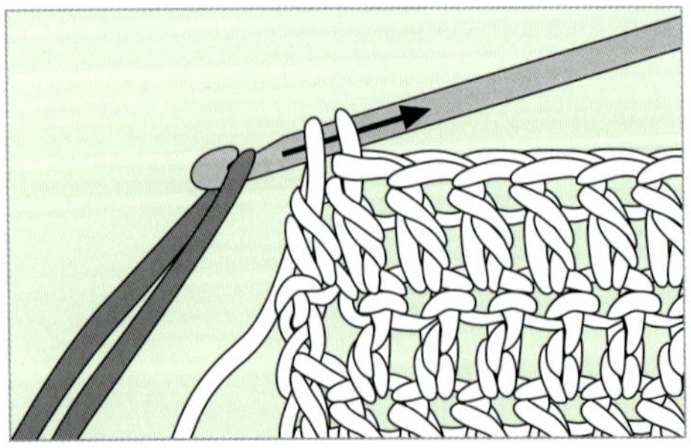

FREE LOOPS OF A CHAIN

When instructed to work in free loops of a chain, work in loop indicated by arrow ***(Fig. 2)***.

Fig. 2

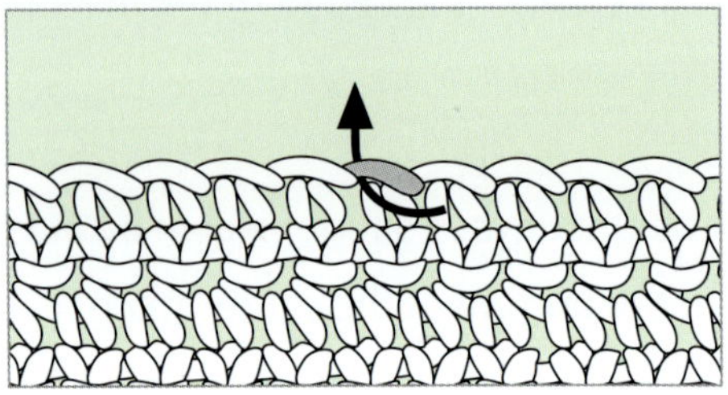

HINTS

As in all crocheted pieces, good finishing techniques make a big difference in the quality of the piece. Make a habit of taking care of loose ends as you work. Thread a yarn needle with the yarn end. With **wrong** side facing, weave the needle through several stitches, then reverse the direction and weave it back through several stitches. When ends are secure, clip them off close to work.

WASHING AND BLOCKING

For a more professional look, Afghans should be washed and blocked. Using a mild detergent and warm water and being careful not to rub, twist, or wring, gently squeeze suds through the Afghan. Rinse several times in cool clean water. Roll Afghan in a clean terry towel and gently press out the excess moisture. Lay Afghan on a flat surface and shape to proper size; where needed, pin in place using rust-proof pins. Allow to dry completely.

Meet the Designer:

Becky Stevens made the move from her home state of Pennsylvania to Maryland more than 40 years ago — which was about the time she started crocheting. She's learned so much about the skill since then that she teaches a weekly group in her home and holds an annual workshop at a New York lake resort. Becky says, "I think the most rewarding things about crochet are relaxing with your project and seeing the final result, especially when making a very personal, thoughtful gift."

Other Leisure Arts books featuring Becky's designs include **Baby's Diagonal Aran Afghans** (#5732), **Crochet Car Seat Blankets** (#75469), **Knit Car Seat Blankets** (#75470), **Hats and Scarves for the Family** (#75499), **Cozy Fashion Accents** (#6658), **Tunisian Dishcloths** (#6371), and **Panel by Panel Afghans** (#4814).

See these books for more of Becky's great designs.

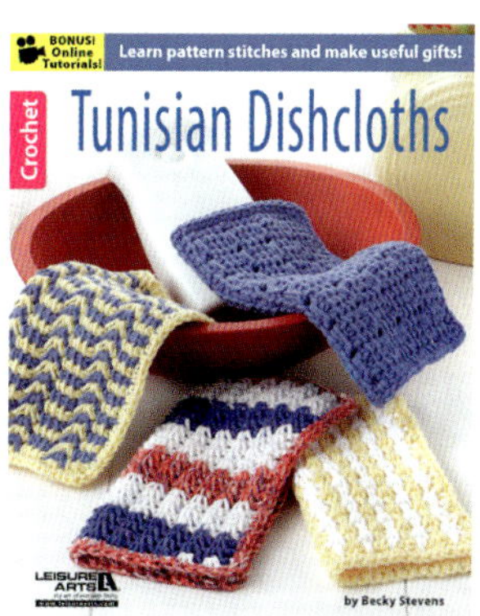

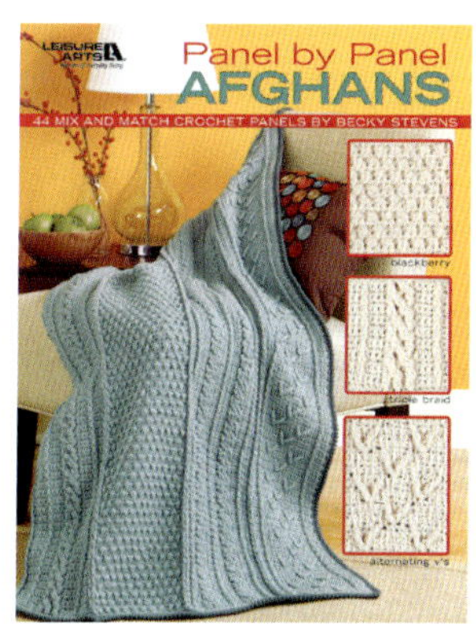

Yarn Information

The Baby Afghans in this book were made using a variety of yarn weights. Any brand of the specified weight of yarn may be used. It is best to refer to the yardage/meters when determining how many balls or skeins to purchase. Remember, to arrive at the finished size, it is the GAUGE/TENSION that is important, not the brand of yarn.

For your convenience, listed below are the specific yarn styles and colors used to create our photography models. Because yarn manufacturers make frequent changes in their product lines, you may sometimes find it necessary to use a substitute yarn or to search for the discontinued product at alternate suppliers (locally or online).

PLAYFUL RIPPLE

Bernat® Softee® Baby™

White - #02000 White

Yellow - #02003 Lemon

Green - #02004 Mint

BERRY PATCH

Bernat® Softee® Baby™

Pink - #02001 Pink

White - #02000 White

Lavender - #30185 Soft Lilac

BOUNCING BABY

Caron® Simply Soft®

Off White - #9702 Off White

Lavender - #9756 Lavender Blue

Purple - #9781 Purple

WAFFLED WARMTH

Lion Brand® Pound of Love®

White - #100 White

Lavender - #144 Lavender

Peach - #133 Creamsicle

BABY SHELLS

Caron® Simply Soft®

Gold - #9755 Sunshine

Lt Blue - #9712 Soft Blue

Blue - #9710 Country Blue

BOBBLING ALONG

Bernat® Baby Sport™

White - #21005 Baby White

Lt Blue - #21128 Baby Blue

Peach - #21510 Peach Blossom

GENTLE WAVES

Caron® Simply Soft®

Teal - #9759 Ocean

White - #9701 White

Aqua - #9780 Robins Egg

SWEET MEMORIES

Bernat® Super Value™

Pink - #53417 Peony Pink

White - #07391 White

Aqua - #53730 Cool Blue

Production Team: Instructional/Technical Editor - Linda A. Daley; Editorial Writer - Susan Frantz Wiles; Senior Graphic Artist - Lora Puls; Photo Stylist - Sondra Daniel; and Photographer - Ken West.